MENTALLY
TOUGH
TEENS

DEVELOPING A
WINNING MINDSET

JUSTIN SU'A

PLAIN SIGHT PUBLISHING
AN IMPRINT OF CEDAR FORT, INC.
SPRINGVILLE, UT

ISBN 13: 978-1-4621-1425-2

Published by Plain Sight Publishing, an imprint of Cedar Fort, Inc.
2373 W. 700 S., Springville, UT 84663
Distributed by Cedar Fort, Inc., www.cedarfort.com

LIBRARY OF CONGRESS CATALOGING-IN-PUBLICATION DATA

Su'a, Justin, 1982- author.
  Mentally tough teens : developing a winning mind set / Justin Su'a.
    pages cm
  Includes bibliographical references and index.
  Summary: Principles that will help youth get through their teenage years and beyond.
  ISBN 978-1-4621-1425-2 (alk. paper)
  1. Youth--Life skills guides. 2. Youth--Conduct of life. I. Title.

  HQ796.S883 2014
  305.235'5--dc23

                         2014004410

Cover design by Angela D. Baxter
Cover design © 2014 by Lyle Mortimer
Edited and typeset by Daniel Friend

Printed in the United States of America

10 9 8 7 6 5 4 3 2 1

Printed on acid-free paper

TO THE YOUTH AROUND THE WORLD. WE'RE COUNTING ON YOU TO BE GREAT.

INTRODUCTION

One of the most awkward yet most awesome moments of my mental coaching career came when a graduating senior gave me a hug and said, "I don't need you anymore." I smiled and told him how proud of him I was. At first, you might think, "What a mean thing to say to someone!" But the reality is, my job as a mindset coach is to help my students help themselves. He and I had been working together for years, and during our time together, he learned how to strengthen his confidence, increase his motivation, and bounce back from hard times.

I don't know why you picked this book up, but I know why I wrote it: to help you develop the mindset necessary for success in whatever you do. Whether you're an athlete, student, musician, or dancer, the tips found in these pages are aimed to help you get out of your own way.

You are living in what some call "the decade of decisions." Within the next ten years, you're going to be making choices that will shape the rest of your life: universities to attend, majors to study, jobs to take, places to move to, the person to marry, how many kids to have, and so on. The best way to plan for the future is to create it, and the best place to start is with yourself. My aim is not to help you *feel* better but to help you *be* better. Good luck on your journey to the great things that lie ahead!

WIN THE MORNING.

What would life be like if you woke up on purpose, with purpose every day? How can you expect to achieve excellence when the first decision you make each day is hitting the snooze button? Win the morning by waking up earlier than you normally do to get a workout in, feed your mind with good books, and fuel your body with a good breakfast—all before the rest of the world is deciding whether to get up or not. Win the morning, and you'll win in life.

SHIFT YOUR
MINDSET.

You are surrounded by peers who want the fastest and easiest path to success, but you don't want that—not anymore. Rather than running from challenges, stare them in the face. Learn about them and embrace them. "The road to greatness is easy," said no one ever. Doing hard things will teach you lessons you wouldn't learn otherwise, and it will make you stronger than you thought possible. You can do this.

EMBRACE
FEEDBACK.

The average person hates to be told what they are doing wrong or what they can do better. Learning to accept feedback isn't easy, but once you decide to seek it out and act on it, you will dramatically improve your progress. Embracing feedback doesn't mean to do what everyone tells you. Identify key mentors or coaches who are great at what they do and, more important, who care about your future. Then allow them to take you places you couldn't have gone otherwise.

TAKE INITIATIVE.

If you see a need, fill it. If you walk by trash, pick it up and throw it away. Be a go-getter. Do things without being told to. Others might think you're trying to suck up, but you know your motives. You're doing things to become better and to help others become better. You don't need others to notice your hard work because you're not doing it for them—you're doing it for you.

LEARN FROM FAILURE.

No one likes to fail, lose, or mess up, but high performers use adversity to learn lessons and refuse to allow setbacks to disable them emotionally. Average teens do everything in their power to avoid failure, even to the extent of living so cautiously that they avoid taking risks. One thing that is inevitable in this life is this: you will fail. But the key is to fail forward. You do this by identifying what you did well, what you can do better, and what you are going to do about it right now.

CHOOSE YOUR ATTITUDE.

One of the most important decisions you make every day is the attitude you are going to have when you walk out your door. Don't take your attitude for granted, or it will get the best of you.

DO ONE MORE.

As an athlete, you can do ten reps in the weight room or you can do eleven. As a musician, you can choose to practice for thirty minutes or thirty-one. One of the best ways to build mental strength is to do something you might not want to do but that you know will help you. Do one more—because the average teenager won't.

KNOW YOUR WHY.

The more clearly you can see your target, the more likely you are to hit it. Mentally tough teens don't do things "just because"; they do things intentionally. When you know why you do what you do, you'll have more power to do it.

GET YOUR PRIORITIES STRAIGHT.

One reason average teens don't achieve their goals is because they allow the things that don't matter to distract them from the things that do. Every day, recommit to the things that matter most. You empower yourself when your priorities are in line.

DON'T EXPECT
IMMEDIATE
SUCCESS.

Success is made in a slow cooker, not a microwave. High-performing teens understand that "overnight" success really comes after years of hard work. Be patient with yourself, keep your eyes on the prize, and focus on the process. The results will take care of themselves.

REFUSE TO ALLOW PEOPLE TO INTIMIDATE YOU.

You don't need anyone's permission to do something great. Putting others on a pedestal because of their talent, experience, and or accolades can make you feel that you're not as good as they are. Anyone can be beat, including your idols, so respect your competition but refuse to fear them.

BE FREE.

Don't sabotage yourself before you attempt something. The words you say matter, and if you think, *I'm going to miss* before you shoot a basketball, *I'm going to fail* before you take a test, or *I'm not going to make it* before you try out for a team, you're already shooting yourself in the foot. If you're going to do something, do it. You don't need to protect your ego by giving others a heads-up of how bad you think you are. The more you're willing to fail, the less likely you are to sabotage yourself before you even try.

GET SOME SLEEP.

It's hard to perform well if you're not sleeping well. I know it's hard, but getting a good night's rest is largely in your hands. For most teens, technology is the biggest thing stopping them from getting optimal sleep. Get off the video games, stop texting, and don't tempt yourself by charging your phone next to your bed; both you and I know you'll be on it all night. If you sleep better, you'll begin to feel better.

THINK STRONG.

Your confidence is something you must take into your own hands. What you say to yourself is more important than what anyone else says to you or about you. Fill your mind with thoughts, words, memories, and goals that empower you, not ones that work against you. Don't undermine your confidence by allowing destructive thoughts to freely enter you mind.

DON'T DO IT BECAUSE IT'S POPULAR.

Don't let the drama of high school distract you from the great things you are going to accomplish in the future. Your peers may have the tendency to care so much about fitting in that they do things to please others instead of doing what's right. Keep in mind that you won't be in your current circumstance forever. It's going to end, and the person you are going to be when it's all said and done should be the person that you intended on being. Champions are willing to go against the grain even when it's not popular.

FOCUS ON WHAT YOU CAN CONTROL.

It's easy to get caught up in who's bigger, stronger, faster, smarter, or better looking than you. The key is to focus on what you can control. You'll never be able to change other people, so instead of worrying about them, focus on yourself. Create the habits you need to be successful in the future. Strive to give your best effort. These things are always in your control.

CREATE SUCCESS ROUTINES.

You've heard that success is a habit. Habits form from routines. Creating a routine is a key strategy elite athletes use to succeed in sports. Now it's your turn to do the same and intentionally create some habits that will benefit you throughout your life. Identify the things that help you feel successful and the things that get in the way of your success. Then create routines based on that information. Start with what you do first thing in the morning, continue with a routine for when you come home from school, and finish with what you do before you sleep at night.

CALM YOUR NERVES.

Feeling anxious? It's not because of the big test, the important game, running for office, or asking that person out on a date. Anxiety comes from the way you're interpreting the situation. Learn to calm your nerves by changing the way you're looking at your circumstance: "What can I learn from this situation?" "What did I do to prepare for this moment?" "How is this going to make me stronger?" "When have I accomplished something difficult in my life before?"

DO THINGS ON
PURPOSE.

Don't you hate being forced to do things? When you feel you have to do something, your motivation tends to dip. Own your motivation by attaching a purpose to everything you do. Developing the habit of thinking, speaking, and acting on purpose and with purpose will help you take the driver's seat of your own life and reap the benefits of acting rather than being acted upon.

MAKE SUCCESS A CHOICE.

You can choose your thoughts, words, and actions. You empower yourself the moment you take decisions into your own hands. Are you struggling right now? My question to you is simple: What are you going to do about it?

REALIZE YOUR CONFIDENCE IS UNDER ATTACK.

Many of these confidence assassins will come in the form of people you love—friends, coaches, and teachers—and many of them don't realize the power their words have on you! Protect your confidence by developing a strong inner voice that says *I can* when others say you can't and *stay strong* when others say give up. Your voice is the one you'll be living with the rest of your life. Respect it. Develop it. Trust it.

FACE FAILURE.

If you view failure as something you are instead of something that happens, then doing difficult things is going to terrify you. Do yourself a favor and learn how to see failure as an opportunity to learn instead of evidence that you're not good enough. Once you can act courageously in the face of fear, you become dangerous.

BE A LEADER.

You need to ask yourself, "Am I making those around me better?" If the answer is no, it's time to step up your game. Mentally tough teens understand that one of their most important attributes is the ability to bring out the best in others. You don't have to be vocal, bubbly, or the next class president; just make a focused effort to have a positive impact on your team, your group of friends, and your family. Don't just take up space—make an impact.

LIVE IN THE
PRESENT.

Refuse to allow the failures of yesterday and the worries of tomorrow keep you from being your best self today. You can't do anything about the mistakes you made last game. You can't take back the words you said last week. You can't undo the bad choices you made last year or protect yourself from never messing up again. But don't let those things stop you. What you do today is what matters most, so focus on being the best version of you in the here and now.

FINISH WHAT YOU START.

Do yourself a favor and commit to finishing what you start. Too many teenagers today day are flakes. Don't you hate it when friends say they are going to do something but never do it? Tell yourself that, no matter how long it takes and no matter how hard it is, you're going to finish. You destroy your ability to trust yourself when you don't do what you say you're going to do, so master the art finishing.

BE YOUR #1 FAN.

Your opinion about yourself is what matters most. You've heard that you are your own worst critic, but make sure you are also your own number one fan. You will meet people who will make you feel special and people who make you feel like dirt. Some will tell everyone how great you are and some will tell everyone how horrible you are. Hold yourself accountable, challenge yourself to get better, and allow yourself to change.

DO IT NO MATTER WHAT.

You're going to find many reasons not to do something—your teacher is boring, the weather is bad, you're not good, and so on. Show up, shut up, and never give up. You'll be happy that you did.

BE RIGHT HERE RIGHT NOW.

You're always at your best when you're in the present. When you quiet your mind and focus on this serve, this note, this test question, and this moment, you'll be more relaxed and more likely to be your best self.

BELIEVE YOU WILL SUCCEED.

Success starts in your mind. It's hard to perform at a high level when you can't even envision yourself being successful. The stronger your belief is in yourself, the more willing you are to push through adversity and uncertainty. And one of the best ways to strengthen your belief in yourself is to prepare diligently.

GIVE MORE THAN YOU RECEIVE.

It's important to understand that sometimes the only thing you will get for your best effort is a thank-you. You shouldn't always expect money, credit, or some other reward for doing something. Learn to give something just because it's the right thing to do. There's nothing wrong with working hard for the sake of working hard. You might get frustrated when all of your efforts go unnoticed, but don't worry; in the process, you were most likely changed for the better.

EXPECT
EXCELLENCE
FROM YOURSELF.

You don't need a parent or a coach to bring out the best in you—bring it out of yourself. Don't be afraid to raise the bar on what you expect from yourself. You can focus a little better, put forth more effort, and bounce back faster on your own, but it's got to be because you want to do it. Greatness is not attained by walking the road of mediocrity. You aren't here to be average. You're here to be great—and greatness is a decision.

DESTROY BAD HABITS.

The person you're going to be in the future will be the result of the habits you form today. Anything great was built one brick, stone, brush stroke, or note at a time, and the same goes for your life—you build a great life by developing habits that lead to success. If you're being held captive by habits that strangle your control, you can break free! With tremendous work, patience, and help from others, bad habits can be broken, and freedom can be restored. Identify a habit that is holding you back and commit today to rip it out of your life.

OWN YOUR JOURNEY.

What drives you? What do you love doing? Follow your passion and stick with it. Don't underestimate how long it will take or how hard it will be, but make sure it's your journey, not a journey someone else wants you to take. Sometimes your final destination may require an unexpected detour. Sometimes the destination might change altogether. Regardless of where you are on your journey, keep your head up and keep moving your feet.

FACE YOUR FEARS.

Fear is one of the most paralyzing emotions a person can feel. You've probably experienced the fear of looking bad, messing up, not doing well on a test, talking to someone you like, or disappointing your parents—that's normal! We all have fears, but mentally tough teens respond differently than your average person. Fear comes from focusing on what's going to happen to you, but courage comes from focusing on what you're going to do about it. What are you afraid of today? Whatever it is, look that fear in the face and then give your attention to what action steps you are going to take.

TAKE A CHANCE.

Is there something you're procrastinating right now? If so, remember that hockey legend Wayne Gretzky once said, "You miss 100 percent of the shots you don't take." Just because you've never been able to do something doesn't mean you can't do it! If you're not taking that leap of faith because you could fail miserably, well, I've got news for you—you're right! I'm not saying that it feels great to fail, but it will definitely make you stronger if your respond properly. You're not going to make an impact by playing it safe. Take some risks. Chances are, you have some untapped potential inside of you that will reveal itself when the pressure is on.

BE PREPARED.

Being prepared is one of the best ways to experience peace of mind. You can't expect to feel confident going into your game, audition, competition, or test if you didn't pay the price of preparation. The keys to preparation are to start early, be consistent, and stay focused. Preparing for tomorrow's big moment will require sacrifice today. It might even mean giving up what you want right now for what you want the most.

LET GO.

You've probably heard many people tell you to "never give up," and in certain circumstances that's great advice. However, sometimes giving up is exactly what you need to do. Give up on trying to be perfect, give up on expecting people to treat you exactly the way you want to be treated, and give up on thinking that you're not good enough. If you're not soaring on the wings of potential that everyone says you have, it might not be because your lack of ability. It just might be because you're allowing yourself to be weighed down by negative people and beliefs—let them go.

MAKE YOUR ACTIONS SPEAK LOUDER THAN YOUR WORDS.

You might tell people that you want to be a professional athlete, musician, or actor. Your heart might be set on going to a certain college or pursuing a certain profession, but do your actions match your desires? Does what you do reflect what you want? First, identify what you want and what it takes to get there. Then be relentless in doing what's necessary to make that happen. If you really want it, you'll find a way. If not, you'll find an excuse.

LISTEN TO YOUR MOM AND DAD.

Your parents might not be as cool as your friends' parents, but remember, they want you to have a better life than they did, and they see more potential in you than you might see in yourself. Do your absolute best to remember that they were there from the beginning. They saw you take your first steps and say your first words, and they did everything they possibly could to put you in a position to succeed. They will live on through you—strengthen your relationship with them.

TAKE A TIME-OUT.

In sports, when the pressure is on and there is little time left, coaches will call a time-out to give their team the game plan, slow down the momentum, and offer some words of encouragement. Great athletes know that when the game speeds up, that's the perfect time to slow down. Same thing in life! If you find yourself buried in homework assignments, practice, rehearsals, church obligations, and other activities, rather than speeding up, slow down. You might be saying to yourself, "I'm too busy to take a time-out!" My response is simple: you can't afford *not* to.

DEVELOP TOUGH SKIN.

Don't take it personally if someone gives you a mean look or yells at you. To be honest, many coaches, teachers, and even parents don't know how to effectively express their feelings, so they revert to uncontrolled yelling. Don't let the intensity and the volume of their words intimidate you. Listen to *what* they are saying, not *how* they are saying it. If they care enough to correct you, make certain that you care enough to learn.

DEBATE YOUR NEGATIVE THINKING.

You won't achieve greatness if you keep telling yourself how bad, ugly, or dumb you are. Just like winning a debate with a sibling or a friend, you've got to do the same thing with your own negative thoughts. Pay close attention to those negative thoughts, then fight back with positive ones. Rather than thinking, *I'm not a good test taker*, you can think, *I may have struggled with tests in the past, but I've paid the price and studied a lot to be prepared for this one.* Instead of saying to yourself, "This person is better than me; what's the use?" you can say, "While it's true that this person may look better than me on paper, I'm not going to let that bother me. I'm going to focus on giving my absolute best and let the results take care of themselves." What you say to yourself matters more than what anyone else can say to you.

STOP
COMPLAINING.

Want to take your mental toughness to the next level? Rip complaining to shreds. Instead of getting mad that you have to do more homework, take a deep breath and get after it. Rather than complaining about how bad your situation is, do something about it. Complaining is a poison that will lead to excuses for a poor performance. You can do a lot more than you think you can, and once you quiet that inner whiner, you'll find that you can do great things.

ACCEPT THAT YOU'RE GOING TO LOSE.

I hope this isn't a shocker to you, but not only are you going to lose, but you also might lose badly. You might lose against someone you should beat, you might lose after you are winning, you might lose in front of many people, and you might even lose so much that you don't win a single time—not even once. If this happens, just know that you aren't alone. One thing all successful people have in common is this: they get up more times than they get knocked down. There is no failure, only feedback. Learn your lessons and do it again.

BE HUMBLE.

The best way to fail is to stop learning. Every great athlete, doctor, musician, or dancer has a teacher or coach. Even superheroes have mentors. Don't let yourself think you are so good that you can't get better. Coaches, parents, peers, and other people who care for you are going to offer advice to help you grow. Some of the things they say might require you to make changes. On some occasions, those changes are going to be painful and will require a lot of work, but remember, it's to make you better. You might not see how the changes are helping you at first, but be patient and trust the process.

PRACTICE WITH PURPOSE.

When the pressure is on, your habits will be revealed. You can't expect to succeed while everyone is watching if you failed to prepare when no one was watching. When you start each practice, have a mission. Identify exactly how you want to improve. If you train yourself with purpose, you can trust yourself in action.

CARRY YOURSELF LIKE A CHAMPION.

Body language is one of the key indicators of a confident person. The way you carry yourself can impact the way you feel about yourself. If you need a little confidence boost, pick your head up, keep your shoulders back, and walk with purpose.

YOU DON'T NEED YOUR "A-GAME."

Don't believe the lie of thinking you need your best stuff to be successful. It doesn't matter if your coach yelled at you, if your opponent is better than you, if the field you're playing on is horrible, or if you're hurt. You can win with your B-game. When you believe in your ability to grind it out, there are no opponents too tough, no classes too difficult. Not a day will go by that you don't compete.

REMEMBER THAT TODAY IS TEMPORARY.

It doesn't matter if you're on top of the world or if you've hit rock bottom, you've got to remember that today doesn't last forever. The best way to avoid getting complacent during success or hitting the panic button during a slump is to remind yourself of these three words: "This is temporary."

REALIZE THAT IT'S ALL ABOUT THE JOURNEY.

The key to success is to focus on the process and let the results take care of themselves. You lose a sense of control when you are fixated on the score, stats, or grades; this will only increase your stress levels. Focus on yourself and what you're going to do right now.

TELL YOUR STORY.

You are a result of the story you keep telling yourself. You'll never succeed if your story is, "I'm not good enough." You'll rarely be victorious if your story is, "I crumble under pressure." Your story can be, "I may not be the best, but I always find a way to compete," or, "Even though I don't have a lot of support, I know what I'm doing is right." Mentally tough teens focus through the distractions and own their own story—even when it's hard.

DON'T GIVE PEOPLE POWER OVER YOU.

Spoiler alert: people are going to treat you differently than you want to be treated. Refuse to allow that to stop you from performing your best. The moment you allow someone to disable you emotionally, you've given them power. Don't do this. If you have, take your power back. It takes tremendous mental and emotional strength to let go and move on, but you can do it; you're on a mission, and you're not going to let anything stop you.

IDENTIFY YOUR SOURCE OF STRENGTH.

Identify the things that give you the strength to endure hard times and keep moving forward. When you want to give up, reflect on these things. Your faith, family, and hope for the future will help you take one more step, try one more time, and get up for one more fight.

LEARN AS MUCH AS YOU CAN.

Be a sponge and soak up as much information as you possibly can. One of the best ways to learn is to pay attention to others' experiences. You don't have to make the same mistakes as your teammates; learn from theirs. You don't have to reinvent the wheel; find out what successful people are already doing. The more you learn, the more confidence you will have.

BE DETERMINED.

You've got to be willing to endure hard and boring things. Have the determination to see things through to completion. You live in a world where many of your peers do something until the next best thing comes around. Develop the ability to grind it out even when you don't want to.

GO DOWN SWINGING.

You won't win if you don't play. You might find yourself in a situation where you can't win, but that shouldn't stop you from making the best attempt you can. When you're the underdog, you work hard and aren't afraid to lose—that makes you dangerous.

BE TRUE TO YOURSELF.

There is no reason to allow people to get you to do things you don't want to do. On many occasions, the right thing and the hardest thing are the same. The only person you'll be living with for the rest of your life is yourself. Being true to yourself will allow you to trust yourself when you need it most.

SEE IT BEFORE YOU DO IT.

If you can paint a clear picture of what you want in your mind, form an unshakable belief that you can do it, and create actions and behaviors to get you there, you'll be amazed at what you can do! The mind is a very powerful tool—use it wisely.

MAKE A DIFFERENCE.

Is your team better because you're a part of it? Do you make a positive impact on the people you see every day? If not, why? One of the most rewarding things you can do is forget yourself and focus on others. How others remember you is the legacy you'll leave behind.

DON'T TAKE THE
EASY ROAD.

The easy road is crowded, filled with many of your complaining, impatient, and unambitious peers. If you want to soar, you've got to take the higher ground. Just like anything that's higher, it requires climbing the high road. The view is better at the top, but it's more difficult to get there. Whatever your situation is right now, I challenge you to either find a way or make a way to the road less traveled. You'll thank yourself later.

AVOID PARALYSIS BY ANALYSIS.

Having too many options can stop you dead in your tracks. In sports, stopping to think about your best option can even cost your team the game! Train yourself to trust yourself. Having a plan A, B, C, and so on can actually impede you from committing to plan A. Keep things simple: make a decision, then commit to it.

CHOOSE A TARGET

Imagine that you and a friend get into a car and start driving (if you're at least sixteen years old of course!). After a few miles, your friends asks, "Where are we going?" and you respond, "I have no idea." This would be a waste of time, gas, and money! Doing something without a purpose or direction is just like that. The best way to reach a destination is to know where that destination is, and the same is true with life. You do yourself a huge favor when you know where you're headed. I'm not saying that you have to plan out your entire life, but at least have an idea of what you want to achieve this month or week. Your motivation will increase when you have something to look forward to.

DO NOT CHEAT.

Don't let your desire to be the best tempt you to take the low road of cheating. It's not worth it. If you're willing to cheat on your homework, then you're willing to cheat on other things. Good grades and athletic victories don't need to come at the price of your integrity. Take the lower grade, lose the point, let someone else have the spot—cheating will never make you better.

TELL YOURSELF YOU CAN.

You can do great things. You can train yourself to relax under pressure. You can continue to learn, grow, and develop into the person you desire to be. You can overcome obstacles, bounce back from failures, and quiet your critics. You can do this.

KNOW IT'S NOT TOO LATE.

The best time to start developing high-performance habits was when you were younger; the second-best time is right now. It's not too late to create new behaviors and eliminate old ones. You're not too old, and it's not too late to begin reinventing yourself.

USE YOUR PRECIOUS TIME WELL.

There are 86,400 seconds in a day, and once they're gone, you can't do anything to retrieve them. So manage them wisely. What you do when you have nothing to do separates the high performers from the average ones. Take advantage of now.

PLAY TO WIN.

Don't let playing for fun be your excuse for not believing you can win. You are growing up in a day where people are getting trophies just for participating and everyone is telling you "good job" to stoke your ego. The reality is that there are winners and losers. Losing is something that happens, but don't let it define who you are. Play to win and when you do, it will make your opponent have to do the same.

WALK IN THE DARK.

For reasons far beyond your control, there will be moments of uncertainty and darkness. Keep walking. Actively wait for the smoke to settle by continuing to move in the direction you want to go. Not seeing is no excuse for not doing.

RECOMMIT DAILY.

Just like brushing your teeth every day, you need to recommit daily to what matters most. It's easy to get distracted in this Twitter-, Facebook-, and Instagram-infested world. You lose power when your priorities are out of line. Taking a look in the mirror to remind yourself of what you want and what you're willing to do to get it is a high-performance habit that will keep you on track.

BE RESPONSIBLE.

Start developing a sense of independence now. Be responsible for your thoughts, actions, emotions, and your future. You don't need Mom and Dad to hold your hand anymore; if you have a problem with your coach, go talk to him. If you have questions about your test, go talk to your teacher. Take matters into your own hands.

GIVE IT YOUR BEST EFFORT.

Not feeling your best is no excuse for not giving your best. If you continue to give your best, your best will continue to get better. There are many things that you have no control over, but your effort level is not one of them. Sprint to the finish line in whatever you do.

AVOID THE DESTROYING POWER OF BUT.

Many of your hopes and dreams won't even have time to develop in your mind if you're full of reasons why you can't achieve them. You might say, "I want to go to that college, but I don't think I can get in," or, "I want to play [insert sport] at the next level, but I don't think I'm good enough." That simple "but" is tempting you to settle for mediocrity and hide behind your fears. Take away the power of that three-letter word by focusing on what you can do, not what you can't.

NEVER BE SATISFIED.

Wherever you are in your life, remind yourself that you can be better. It doesn't matter if you're at the top of your game or experiencing a terrible slump—things can get better. Stay hungry for knowledge, thirsty for improvement, and dedicated to becoming more than you are today.

HOLD ON.

There will come a time in your teenage years that the only thing you'll be able to do is hold on. There will be moments where you feel like life is chewing you up and spitting you out. Friends will turn into foes, injuries may ruin your career, and windows of opportunity might close for good. Carry on by asking yourself two questions: "How is this experience making me stronger?" and "What can I learn from what I'm going through?" If you're being required to go through a tough time, you might as well use it to better yourself.

ACCEPT THAT THERE ARE NO GUARANTEES.

You aren't entitled to success. Championships, honor rolls, and other accolades are not given—they are earned. Thinking you can achieve great things without paying the price is crazy! And even if you do work hard, the results you desire are not guaranteed. The next time is not guaranteed. Not even tomorrow is guaranteed, so make the most of this moment and embrace today.

FIND THE POWER TO SAY NO.

Motivation is the engine that drives your performance. When you discover your purpose for doing what you do, it will also give you the power to confidently say *no* to the behaviors that are holding you back, the people who cause you to lose focus, and the distractions that are wasting your time. Your motivation will give you a reason to be courageous.

LEAN ON YOUR FAN CLUB.

You're going to hit a time of complete exhaustion. You will think that you can't do another assignment, run another lap, attend another practice, or read another page. When you've hit the wall and you want to throw in the towel, remember your fan club. Your fan club consists of the people who love you regardless of your success or failure. Your fan club might include your family, your best friend, a coach, or someone from church. Sometimes, when you're running on empty, the love of others can carry you until you're back on your feet.

USE THE MIRROR TEST.

The hardest test you'll ever have to take is the one where you look yourself in the mirror and ask, "What am I doing with my life?" "Am I living up to my potential?" "Am I in control of my own life?" "What's holding me back from being better than I am today?" "Do I know what I want, and am I acting on it every day?" If you don't like any of your answers, then ask, "What am I going to do about it?" Only you can answer these questions, and if you're honest, this can be a test that will change you forever.

PROTECT
YOURSELF.

You can be your own worst enemy. Guard your mind from limiting beliefs that cause you to shrink and not hold your head high. Comparing yourself to a teammate who has been playing the sport for many years longer than you can hurt your confidence. Using your friends' strengths as the measuring stick to your weakness is a sure way to fill your mind with doubt. The person who is going to do the most damage to your mind and heart is you—protect yourself from yourself.

REMEMBER THAT YOU'RE NOT THE ONLY ONE.

You aren't the only one with goals. There are thousands of other teenagers just like you who want to go to the college you are applying to. Dozens of other athletes are vying for the same position you are. Hundreds of other students are also trying to get scholarships. There's no time to get complacent. Keep in mind that if you stop hustling, someone else is still going.

EMBRACE THE PAIN.

It's not easy to be successful. It can be painful to sacrifice sleep to work out before school. It can be painful to choose to not go out with your friends so you can practice a little longer. It can be painful to push your body to the limits. Pain is a part of growth and is necessary for success.

BE CAREFUL WHAT YOU MEASURE.

Measuring the wrong things can lead to negative thinking. Comparing yourself to others can cause you to beat yourself up. Realizing that where you are now is nowhere near where you want to be can lead to frustration. Instead of measuring how many pounds you want to lose, count how many days you go to the gym in a row. Rather than using your performance results as your only standard, keep track of how many hours you spend practicing your craft. If you want to see progress, base your success on what you do today.

BE NICE.

You never know what others are going through, so be kind. When you have confidence in yourself, you'll have the ability to walk though the halls of your school with your head up and look your peers in the eye. Don't mistake kindness for weakness, and don't think kindness is about putting on a cheesy smile and acting fake. It's really about paying attention to what others might be going through and to what you can do to help raise them to higher ground.

KEEP YOUR EYES ON THE PRIZE.

When adversity arises, the mentally weak will focus on the struggle and take their eyes off the prize. You started down this road for a reason; remember your goals for this journey. Keep in mind all of the people who are supporting you and the satisfaction of doing what others said you couldn't do. Remember your reasons, and your excuses will fall to the side.

CONTROL YOUR MIND.

What you feed grows. This is a principle of the mind. Where you choose to put your thoughts will have a tremendous impact on your performance, so choose wisely. Train your mind to find the diamonds in the rough, look for possibilities, and focus on solutions. If you want to start changing what you do, start changing what you think.

BE DISCIPLINED.

Peak performers have the ability to do things others don't feel like doing. You can't expect to win games, get good grades, or make the team if you're only willing to practice on the days you feel good. Have the discipline to work through boredom. Focus on quality over quantity. Do what you say you are going to do, even if you don't feel like doing it.

GO ALL IN.

Going all in means that you are willing to do more than what is expected without worrying about what you look like in the process. Many teens are afraid to go all in because they think, *What if it doesn't work out?* They hold back from giving their best because if they fail, at least they can protect their ego by saying, "I didn't try my hardest." If you're focused on the results, going all in can look like a risky thing, but the truth is that there's no risk at all. When you go all in, there is one thing that is guaranteed—you'll come out the other side with a clear conscience, knowing that you gave everything you had.

MAKE FRIENDS.

Be careful not to allow school cliques to keep you from making more friends. It's easy to get caught into thinking that you "shouldn't" talk to someone because of who they hang out with, what grade they're in, or what team they play on. There is a proverb that says, "Life is like chess—the king and the pawn eventually go back into the same box." Understand that your best efforts to make friends might not work, and people might treat you badly.

IMPROVE LITTLE BY LITTLE.

As the saying goes, "Life is a game of inches." The mentally tough teen understands the power of the little things: a simple athletic drill, a monotonous task, and a seemingly unimportant assignment all add up to something greater. When you find yourself in a position where people are counting on you to be great, your confidence will be a result of all the little things you did day in and day out. Fight for every little inch of improvement, even if it's only for 1 percent better. And remember the Tanzanian proverb, "Little by little, a little becomes a lot."

KNOW THE DIFFERENCE BETWEEN A PRIVILEGE AND A RIGHT.

Going through driver's education, you might hear your instructor say, "Driving is a privilege and not a right." In other words, it's something that you *get* to do and not something that is *owed* to you. Keep yourself grounded by remembering that no one owes you anything. Count going to school, playing your sport, and being a member of your team as a privilege and as an opportunity to get better. This mindset precedes gratitude, and when you work hard and stay humble, great things happen.

GET RID OF THE HAVE TO MINDSET.

Don't you hate being forced to do something? You may have thought, "I *have* to go to practice," "I have to write this essay," or "I *have* to lose weight." Usually when you feel that you *have* to do something, your motivation to do it and enjoyment of doing it go way down. The next time you *have* to do something, change the language to *get to*. Try this on for size: "I *get* to go to practice," "I *get* to write this essay," or "I *get* to lose weight." Having the *get to* mindset does a very important thing—it puts the power back in your hands.

GET COMFORTABLE BEING UN-COMFORTABLE.

One of the key characteristics of a mentally tough person is the ability to be comfortable being uncomfortable. Decide that you will not be like the average person, complaining when things aren't working out the way you'd like them to. You will be faced with bad weather, a teacher with high standards, or a seemingly insurmountable number of points scored by the other team. The easy thing to do is panic and react negatively, but the mentally tough thing to do is to respond cool, calm, and collectedly. You'll be uncomfortable many times—but if you're expecting that, you can own your situation.

OWN YOUR MISTAKES.

When you don't succeed, avoid playing the blame game. It's easy to give excuses for a poor performance. Have the strength to look in the mirror and take ownership for your failures and shortcomings. Too many teens think the reason they aren't where they want to be is because of bad teaching, coaching, or parenting or a lack of sleep, money, or time. Only when you can say, "It's my fault" are you able to do something about it.

ACCEPT THAT LIFE
IS HARD.

You can't expect to dance through life without losing, experiencing pain, encountering mean people, and feeling lonely, hopeless, or at the brink of giving up. For reasons far beyond your own control, there will be moments of uncertainty and darkness—keep your feet moving. No one ever said life would be easy, but if you react with mental toughness, life will be worth it.

BE REMEMBERED.

Imagine having a banquet at the end of your life with every one of your family members, friends, classmates, teachers, teammates, coaches, opponents, and anyone else you came in contact with during your years on earth. That's a lot of people! Now, imagine having the opportunity listen to what everyone says they remember about you—what do you hope they say? Would they talk about your work ethic? Would they talk about your kindness and determination? Or would they talk about how you gave up easily and complained a lot? Take a look at your life right now. Do your actions match how you want to be remembered?

ACTIVELY WAIT.

You might be worried about not being ready when your window of opportunity arrives or even whether that opportunity is going to come at all. Rather than sit back and wait for something to happen to you, hustle to make it happen. There are going to be things that you will have to be patient for, but "being patient" isn't another way of saying, "sit in your room and play video games until that day arrives." You can actively wait for that moment by preparing yourself to be ready for it when it comes. Take advantage of the quiet before to storm, and you'll have the confidence to stand in the middle of it when it arrives.

GET MENTALLY FIT.

Just like you go to the gym to train your body, you need to take time to condition your mind. Mental toughness is done on purpose. It's training your mind to believe that you can overcome all odds, and it's believing that you can look fear in the face and go after what you want. Training your mind is being aware of the negative thoughts that creep in when you're not paying attention. Your mindset is yours to control— own it.

DON'T KILL YOUR CONFIDENCE.

One way to be your own worst enemy is to attribute your success to something outside of your control. When things work out, don't say, "I got lucky," "The other team just played bad," or "That was just an easy test." When you pawn off your success onto things other than the hard work and effort you put into it, you undermine your confidence! I'm not saying you should be boastful and hog all the credit; of course give credit where it's due, but when you can look at your accomplishment and say, "I did everything I could to achieve that," you will be strengthening your belief in yourself and your confidence to tackle the next difficult thing.

MAKE DEPOSITS IN YOUR CONFIDENCE BANK.

Many people believe confidence comes from winning—but that's false. While it's true that winning can help boost confidence, the best source of confidence comes from a sense of feeling prepared. Preparation comes from caring deeply about the amount of effort and focus you give at practice. Every time you practice or train on purpose and with purpose, you are putting money in your confidence bank. And when the moment arrives where you need that confidence in order to succeed, it will be there because of all of the preparation you put forth earlier.

BE THE DRIVER.

Don't let anyone else assume the driver's seat in your life. In addition to that, don't rely on anyone else to do the driving for you. Keep in mind that you control the gas and brake pedals of your life. If you don't like where you're headed, hit the brakes and change directions. If you're feeling discouraged because you aren't going anywhere, identify where you want to go and hit the gas pedal. You will make a wrong turn here and there, and you'll even be stuck in traffic occasionally, but remember that you are not the passenger; you are the driver, so take control of the wheel.

GAIN STARTING POWER.

If you want to separate yourself from the average person, be willing to start from square one. Many teens hold themselves back from doing something great because they lack the ability to start. Starting from nothing looks difficult when you focus on all the time and effort it's going to take to finish. If you run into this problem, tell yourself why starting right now is better than delaying. Starting today will turn nothing into something through diligent effort.

WORK HARD.

Ask anyone who has achieved something great how they did it, and they will mention hard work. If you want to be better at anything, it's going to take relentless, focused, consistent, unwavering hard work. Be willing to be the first to show up and the last to leave. Have the ability to stick with a task through boredom and sleepiness. Hard work doesn't guarantee good grades, championships, or scholarships, but it puts you in the best possible position to achieve those things. When you work hard, you will change in the process and inspire others along the way.

KNOW WHERE YOU'RE GOING.

When you know where you're going, you're more likely to get there. You might be thinking, *I'm too young to know what I want in the long term.* That's okay, but let me ask you this: What are you going after this year? What do you hope to accomplish this month? What are you looking forward to today? Knowing where you are going doesn't necessarily mean having a clear picture of where you are going to end up, but it does mean creating checkpoints along the way.

HAVE A LAST DAY MENTALITY.

If today were the last day of your life, how would you treat people? How would that impact your priorities? What would that do to the gossip, bullying, and daily drama you experience at school? If this were your last day playing your sport, how would that impact your effort level? Anytime you experience the last of anything, you tend to appreciate it more, dismiss little frustrations, and focus on people rather than on things. Steve Jobs put it well: "Remembering that you are going to die is the best way I know to avoid the trap of thinking you have something to lose."

SURROUND YOURSELF WITH GREATNESS.

Sometimes all it takes is a small spark to light the fire of your soul. Surround yourself with people who will lift you to higher ground—people who are doers, not just talkers. When you are in the presence of greatness, it will make you want to get better, do more, and make positive changes to your life. Have the courage to walk away from those who are pulling you down, even if it requires standing alone.

STAND OUT.

While average teens are doing everything in their power to fit in, the mentally tough teen seeks to stand out. Standing out means you could be ridiculed, bullied, or pushed away, but it can also lead to setting a positive example and inspiring others. Rather than seeking to go unnoticed, master your craft so well that you can't be ignored.

CONSISTENTLY CHOOSE THE
RIGHT.

The greatness you achieve in the future is going to be the result of your ability to make good choices day in and day out. You are faced with decisions every day. Some of them are conscious and some of them are not. Rather than tear yourself up over the bad decisions you've made in the past, choose to make a better one right now. You are a product of the decisions you make every day—remember that the difficult choice and the right choice are often the same thing.

DO MORE THAN IS NECESSARY.

There is a big difference between what you can do and what you're willing to do. The mentally tough teen does the things the average teen isn't willing to. If you're tired of performing beneath your potential, you must do something extra to improve. You can't expect to get outstanding results through a mediocre effort level. Excellence is a choice, and you need to start choosing to do more than what is necessary. Take your mind and body to the next level by making sure your actions match the heights of your expectations.

BE A GREAT TEAMMATE.

Strive to be a contributing member of whatever team you're a part of; it doesn't matter where you play, but how. Pick others up when they fail, cheer them on when they succeed, and do your job the best you can for the benefit of those who are counting on you. When the dust settles and the years have passed, your teammates won't remember how many hits you got, points you scored, or goals you made. They'll remember the kind of person you were.

EMBRACE THE POWER OF INTEGRITY.

Don't worry about doing the right thing for everyone to see. Instead, do the right thing even if no one else finds out. It takes mental toughness to have integrity because it may mean that you wind up with the short end of the stick. Being true to your word, even if it's inconvenient for you, makes you a great teammate, friend, and family member. Be the kind of person others can trust when their backs are turned.

TAKE A DEEP BREATH.

Use this moment to take a nice, slow, deep breath. A deep breath is a great tool for calming your nerves. If you're about to take a difficult test, take a deep breath before each question. About to play in a big game or audition for a play? A deep breath is the answer. It will relax your muscles and quiet your mind. Life happens quickly, so be sure to pump the brakes by slowing down your breathing.

STOP COMPARING YOURSELF TO OTHERS.

You're going to have your bad acne days, and sometimes parts of your body will seem too big or too small. But that's not the worst part—while you're so busy beating up on yourself, you're putting other teens on pedestals, thinking they are "gorgeous," "perfect," or "better" than you. The reality is that they're human too! And chances are that they're comparing their weaknesses to your strengths as well. So before you decide to stay home from school because you can't stand how you look, focus on your strengths. Even better, focus on what you're going to do to make a difference in someone else's life.

RECOGNIZE THAT ATTITUDE IS EVERYTHING.

The attitude you have as you approach the tests you take, the sprints you run, and the classes you have will make a tremendous impact on how you perform. It takes mental toughness to maintain a good attitude despite being in a difficult position. Even if you haven't been able to accomplish something before, a positive attitude is the first step to accomplishing it now.

TAKE ONE THING AT A TIME.

You're setting yourself up for failure if you try to make too many changes at once. The process of making new habits drains your limited supply of willpower. Rather than aiming for a complete makeover (getting fit, going to bed earlier, and being more positive all at once), focus on one goal at a time. It's better to commit to improving one thing and then move on to the next rather than trying to improve many things at once.

APPRECIATE A
FRESH START.

The great thing about life is that it's filled with fresh starts! You have a fresh start on the first day of each year and month. And while everyone else is dreading Monday, you can see it as an opportunity to begin again. Every morning is another chance to reinvent yourself. If you think of each day as a blank slate, you'll feel a great sense of freedom. Make today great; you've never lived it before.

ASK FOR HELP.

There will be many times when you find yourself in a situation that will leave you in the dark. There will be moments when it seems as though you've tried everything, but nothing is working. Asking for help isn't a sign of weakness; it's a sign of being coachable. You don't have to live in quiet desperation. You don't have to suffer alone. Ask for help. Don't think that no one cares, because someone does. Nothing is wrong with you for having problems—everyone does. Get the help you need and conquer your problems.

CARE A LOT.

When you care about something, you don't take it for granted. How you treat people and things depends on how much you care about them. If you care about your future, that will impact how you act today. If you care about your family, then that will help you overcome selfishness. Are you trying to be a better friend? Here's a tip: sincerely care about them.

LOOK FORWARD.

Paint a vivid picture of a bright future and hold on to it. Your parents' life doesn't have to be your life, and what has been the norm for people in you situation doesn't have to be your fate. Many people have survived devastating life storms by holding on to one thought: There will be a better day. Keep your head up, keep your eyes on the prize, and remember that hope is always pointed forward.

ENVISION YOUR POTENTIAL.

Great athletes have the ability to see plays unfold before they actually happen. Successful business professionals are masterful at seeing things happen in their minds years before they really do. Develop the ability to see yourself not as you are today but as the person you can be if you live up to your potential. The lessons you are learning from today's hardships might be preparing you to do great things in the future. Be careful not to jump to conclusions; things might not make sense until later.

PLAY TILL THE WHISTLE.

This is a coaching phrase that means, "Go hard until someone stops you." The same is true in life. Some teens stop because they think the whistle has already been blown and that the game is over, but in reality there is still time left! No matter what happened in your first attempt, keep going until time runs out. If you succeeded at first, you can do even better. If you failed at first, you can still succeed. As long as you have a heartbeat and air in your lungs, you still have time— play till the whistle.

KNOW THAT YOU MATTER.

You'll never have the courage to attack your dreams if you don't feel worthy of them. Why not you? Why not now? Success sees no color, gender, height, age, weight, or ethnicity. Success is accessible to the rich and the poor, the experienced and the beginners. You deserve to give it a shot. You can do this—just take the first step.

SILENCE THE HATERS BY BEING SUCCESSFUL.

You are going to have people who don't like you and talk behind your back. Rather than getting tangled in words of argument and hate, let your life do the talking. Act with poise and control in the face of ridicule. Refuse to give people power over you. After all, "Tigers don't loose sleep over the opinions of sheep."

USE YOUR POWER TO CREATE.

If you're waiting for the perfect time to do something, you're going to be waiting for a long time! You have the power to create opportunities for success, the ability to create friendships that will last a lifetime, and the capacity to create the kind of life that you can be proud of. You are the architect of your future, and you're creating it one day at a time. As Coach John Wooden said, "Make today your masterpiece."

HELP OTHERS MOVE ON.

It takes tremendous mental toughness to move past the mistakes of others. If your friends or teammates make mistakes, it doesn't help to hang those mistakes over their heads. It's very difficult to change, but the process becomes more difficult when you don't allow others to change. Believe you can grow, but also believe that others can as well.

REMEMBER THAT YOU CAN CHANGE.

Refuse to fall into the trap of thinking that the glass is half-empty and that there is nothing you can do about it. You can change, but the lasting change you're looking for is a long process, and you will learn painful lessons along the way. If you find yourself struggling, remember that rock bottom is the perfect place to start building.

ABOUT THE AUTHOR

Justin Su'a is the Head of Mental Conditioning at the IMG Academy, the world-leading provider of athletic and personal development training programs for youth, adult, collegiate, and professional athletes, located in Bradenton, Florida. He's also a member of the Association for Applied Sport Psychology (AASP). He completed his masters in exercise science from the University of Utah with an interest in the nature of peak performance. Justin's students perform in the NFL, Olympics, Dancing With the Stars, Division I universities, and in numerous business corporations. He's also worked with the American Samoa National Olympic Committee and the Unites States Military. Justin was a Freshman All-American Pitcher at Brigham Young University, and he is also the author of *Parent Pep Talks: The 10 Mental Skills Your Child Must Have to Succeed in Sports, School, and Life.*